D1566628

ALL OF THE ABOVE

ALL OF THE ABOVE

JIM DANIELS

Adastra Press
MMXI

Poems from this collection have appeared in the following
periodicals: *Alchemy, Graffiti Rag, Great River Review, Jam
Today, The MacGuffin, Mankato Poetry Review, North American
Review, Puerto Del Sol, Wormwood Review.*

Adastra Press
16 Reservation Road
Easthampton, MA 01027

The poems in *All of the Above* loosely follow
Jim Harrison's definition of ghazals in *Outlyer
and Ghazals*. He writes, "I have not adhered
to the strictness of metrics and structure of the
ancient practitioners, with the exception of
using a minimum of five couplets. The couplets
are not related by reason or logic and their
only continuity is made by a metaphoric jump."
I restricted each of my poems to exactly five
couplets.

—J. D.

1.

One man claims to make rain,
another to find water with a stick.

I threw my dog into the air above the river
expecting him to swim, hoping for flight.

Rain comes down, no getting around it.
It freezes, but it still comes down.

Always a hand reaching out over water.
It is rarely long enough.

A man rows a boat, 6 a.m., in the rain.
No one happier or sadder.

2.

Buddy, he called, *buddy*. Speech oozed out
his infected eye. I knew the rest—kept walking.

I picked at the scab, but still it quickly healed.
No comfort in old scars.

Don't scuff those new shoes. The old familiar *oops*.
Stop hurrying and fix me something good.

You can't get a sunburn from a red moon;
nevertheless, don't stay out too long.

No matter how much I shadowbox,
the gravediggers still blow on their hands.

3.

The thermometer on the porch fell
the day they came to kick my brother's ass.

I never showed up behind the school
where Luckman waited with his friends.

Norman's boots sang down the hall,
a song memorized by Chilton's face.

A rose broke out above one eye, then his nose,
his lips, a bouquet I walked away from.

Kill-the-guy-with-the-ball was our favorite game.
Any ball would do.

4.

Helping with communion, I saw the pale, dry tongues
of nuns no one would ever kiss.

Junior high party, Diane Lacy leans drunk against
the garage, boys shoving marshmallows down her
    pants.

I took Debbie home for lunch while my mother was
    at work.
Afterward in chemistry class, I inhaled my fingers.

At the National Burlesque, strippers gave out hand-
    dipped
cookies to starving men. I kept mine till it crumbled.

I scratched my dresser knobs with the initials of
    dreams.
G for girls. I forget the rest.

5.

A man eats a hot dog in the window
of a passing train. His cheeks bulge.

He looks as happy and mindless as the dog
squinting up, crapping on the brick alley.

We share a certain fondness, like foreigners
nodding to each other on an off-season ferry.

Wildflowers blur in the distance, ghosts
of what I once knew.

Sometimes I fall in love
just watching someone chew gum.

6.

They played with jokers—
jokers ruled everything.

He used his shoelace as a bookmark
until it turned into a lock of hair

that he hugged tight to his chest
till it turned into a strand of spaghetti

and, being hungry, he slurped it up.
I have lost my place, he cried.

Let's make up a place, she said. *Let's name it
after a word in this book,* he said.

7.

I would've kicked his ass, he said.
The bleachers stacked with unhappy couples.

In the next car, they gestured madly.
He slapped her. She turned right on red.

What's sin? He knew the first lines
of all the prayers. His first lines were his best.

He opened and closed his hand like a mouth.
She turned to the window, but the drapes were closed.

He gave me the finger. I had to deck him.
Don't look at me like that. She looked at him like that.

8.

Once driving around a corner on two wheels,
I felt all life tilting toward another world.

A guy I pinned in fifteen seconds in a wrestling meet
shot someone six times last week.

A girl who wiped spaghetti from my face
slipped in spilled gas and went down flaming.

A foaming dog chased me down the street.
I hopped a fence, got down on all fours to snarl back.

When I squished a rat in my driveway
I smiled because it was not a child's head.

9.

I am tired of cracking the same knuckles.
Bring me new hands.

I want to be a sparkler.
At least I am long and thin.

None of us have perfect skins or hands without roads.
Dog bite, wart. Slammed door, burn.

My father's slap. Lynn's sweaty palm under a desk.
I cover my cough. I cover my yawn.

Look at my hands. They are strangers,
and one holds a pen.

10.

An old man in a kayak steers down the river.
We both know the hidden rocks he stays clear of.

Sitting in a tub with you, the curtain circling us,
I want to crawl back in.

Under a rusty bridge, two winos
oxidize against a pylon.

Once I held my breath face-down under water
till you yanked me up.

I can't say where I was going then, what string
I was swimming toward. What hook.

11.

A bald man in a white shirt sits unbuttoned
in his blue car by the river.

A black dog pisses on every tree, rolls over
in something dead, lifts his nose to the sky.

I know a lot of stories about back seats.
Maps never helped me.

A small boy on a swing shouts, a young woman
  pushes,
wind raising her skirt.

Leaves landing in the river whisper secrets.
The repeated cry of a duck is my head nodding.

12.

A hobo costume is easiest. Easier even
than a clown. Easier than a ghost.

We have given the moon a lot of faces.
Maybe it's just a bald spot in that black hair.

*The trouble with Martin is that I think
he wears a beret on the inside too.*

He chose style over warmth. He chose the black crayon.
Don't blame me, blame my bones, he said.

When the last wedge of light slams shut, nothing
will glow in the dark. Do not save your pretty dresses.

13.

He held a radio to his ear, its worn leather case,
the soft skin, the voice of his mother.

The word *memory*, the *mem* part—it jumps off
our lips—we hold on to the rickety ride.

Who is my savior and what will he save me from?
An organ throbbing in a cathedral—who could ask
   for more?

The blind woman wears a plastic bag over her head
during rainstorms. Heaven or purgatory? She is dry.

The poor heart. All it wants
is to keep us alive.

14.

We were intimate as two clowns
after the last show.

When she said *My third husband....*
I wanted her to stop.

He wore his hat backwards—I should have known.
Just a bunch of hair, nothing, bleached skull.

Some roads give you the heebie-jeebies.
Oops is the word on the moon's lips.

I believe in the innocence of open windows.
The confusion of car doors? You can have it.

15.

I'm leaving, she says, *it's over.*
In the tent of his fingers, a prayer sweats it out.

A fat bee crashes against the window.
Another tiny door slams.

His father drew tattoos on his arm: anchor, heart.
The heart anchored, that's what he wants.

Rust turns his hands orange. *Is it worth saving?*
It, their love. He spits into his hands and rubs.

He draws circles around the wart in his palm,
the zero—weightless, adrift.

16.

At the beach a sleeping man's hat says *Mine's bigger
than yours*—his son buries him in sand.

A girl licks a popsicle, squints up, not willing
to share. It melts over her fingers.

A boy ties a towel around his neck, runs
into the water, a superhero with the power to be
  happy.

What chance does he have against his father
brushing off sand, shouting *get back here*?

Metal detectors crackle the loneliness of old men.
A girl quietly loads sand into her bathing suit.

17.

In the stringy shade of a tall willow, girls practice
cheers: step, kick, jump, and fall in weeds.

Behind a garage, boys expose their penises.
A bored dog lies at their feet.

Wind smacks rain into hard beads. A woman
carries laundry in, hugging sheets.

Mail slides from a man's lap to the floor.
He snores over a cold cup of tea.

In the park, a young couple green
on their knees. Porch lights dim, distant.

18.

I remember that smell:
it was cheese I wanted.

I kept my baby teeth in a jar
until I opened it and gagged.

I keep a lucky stone in my pocket.
My luck is I haven't lost it.

I squeeze good moments like clay in my fists.
Sleep, sleep, but it will not fix my crooked teeth.

If life consists of dancing on a guitar string,
give me a fat one.

19.

The box said *Do not tamper* and I tampered.
The wet matches wouldn't light.

A boy longs for lightning.
His mother chases him through rain.

A gust shakes the bushes, night's green ghosts.
Mice in the kitchen tunnel through pudding.

A dog bit me, sensing my fear.
Dead by now. I trace my thin scar.

Wet leaves tongue my skin. Heart beat
under a bridge. Rain circling in.

20.

A kid pushes scratched glasses up his nose,
snuffling tears, sorry again.

Wet dirt around our lips like rain clouds.
Nothing can stop us from becoming mud.

Smudged with regret. Ticking with pleasure.
Soul Eater's Holiday.

Relief in clear glass. Complicated fragments
chanted against prayer.

My mother's cool hand on my forehead
disappearing.

21.

Calm so moist and sedating
I almost floated into my tea.

A green lizard puffed up its red chest
for her. The rams crashed and danced.

He wore a baseball hat to his third wedding
hoping for a better average.

She was so relaxed she took off
her artificial leg.

I lied to the priest about telling lies
to avoid spilling my first erotic dream.

22.

I can't help being pretty, noticing
the chip in every precious cup.

I wish I had red hair and Darlene
didn't die in the fire.

I don't make fun of saints
as long as they stay out of my way.

I threw a ring as far as I could.
Not very far.

In my dreams, old radio stations
crackle with perfection.

23.

Finally, it's about dust kicking up from the road
like a delirious child on its way somewhere delicious.

Some days the world refuses to be a smart-ass
or a smug half-filled coffee mug.

The three lean hipsters smoking a joint on a balcony
across the street have no furniture in their apartment.

I push my thumb through the grapefruit's skin.
My multiple choice answer is *all of the above.*

Under the surprised moon's eye, let us show
a willingness to tremble.

24.

My kite is loose. I chase a ball of string
unraveling in the street.

Village of the Damned was the first
movie I saw with a girl.

By closing my bedroom door until it clicked,
I kept my sick grandmother alive for years.

I once thought I had a lot of power
but it was only a handful of red kisses.

There's only one set of rules:
Hold on. Let go.

COLOPHON

250 copies of
All of the Above by
Jim Daniels of Pittsburgh
were letterpress printed on an
8 x 12 C & P from handset type
with papers hand-fed, -collated, -folded,
and -sewn ❧ Type is Garamond, named for
the sixteenth century French type founder,
with Caslon Open for display ❧ Papers are
Classic Columns Natural White text and Royal
Fiber Driftwood cover with various endsheets;
all the papers are recycled ❧ Design and labor
by Gary Metras at his Adastra Press in Easthamp-
ton, Massachusetts ❧ Production lasted August
to September through Tropical Storm Irene,
flooding, a rainy vacation to Cape Cod,
and the tying of bullet-head grass-
hopper flies to fool late
summer trout
❧